Heavenly Coffee Recipes

Recipes

Spice Up Your Regular Cup of Joe

BY

Stephanie Sharp

Warning - Disclaimer

The purpose of this book is to educate and entertain. The author and does not guarantee that anyone following these techniques, suggestions, tips, ideas, or strategies will become successful. The author shall have neither liability nor responsibility to anyone with respect to any loss or damage caused, or alleged to be caused, directly or indirectly by the information contained in this book.

Thank you so much for purchasing my book! As a reward for your purchase, you can now receive free books sent to you every day. All you have to do is just subscribe to the list by entering your email address in the box below and I will send you a notification every time I have a free promotion running. The books will absolutely be free with no work at all from you!

Who doesn't want free books? No one! There are free and discounted books every day, and an email is sent to you 1-2 days beforehand to remind you so you don't miss out. It's that easy!

Just visit the link or scan QR-code to get started!

https://stephanie-sharp.subscribemenow.com

Table of Contents

Introduction

You don't need to be a professional barista or have training to enjoy delicious macchiatos, smoothies, lattes and more at home. With this book you can enjoy easy, flavourful coffee recipes that will bring your coffee game up a notch... or 10! Enjoy different recipes for frozen and blended coffee, warm coffee, iced coffee, coffee treats and more!

Coffee can be so much more than just your favourite instant coffee mix and some water or a trip to your local coffee shop, you can begin to explore different flavours, aromas and combinations and find some things that you really love and enjoy. Be your own barista and brew your way to taste bud heaven with strong espresso martinis, yummy coffee and walnut cakes and creamy cappuccinos.

Basic Instant Coffee

This recipe stands great on its own in the flavour realm, but it can also be the base for most of the recipes in this book that call for already brewed coffee. You can spice it up in whatever way you like. If a recipe calls for the same ingredients that are already in this mix, simply omit them or add or subtract based on measurements.

Serves: 2

Prep Time: 2 minutes

Instructions:

- 2 cups of hot water
- 2 tablespoons of milk or creamer
- 2 teaspoons of instant coffee
- 2 teaspoons of sugar (adjust to taste)
- 1 teaspoon of vanilla extract

Ingredients:

1. Combine all ingredients and mix well.

Pumpkin Spice Latte

Want to enjoy a dairy free, healthy coffee recipe this holiday season? This recipe is made with delicious pumpkin and has a sweet maple syrup flavour, yum!

Serves: 1

Prep Time: 7 minutes

Ingredients:

- 1 cup of brewed coffee
- ½ cup of almond or cashew milk (divided in half)
- 1 ½ tablespoons of pumpkin puree
- 2 tablespoons of maple syrup
- 1 teaspoon of vanilla extract
- ½ teaspoon of pumpkin pie spice
- A pinch of salt

Ingredients:

1. Combine ingredients in a small saucepan over medium-low heat until mixture is heated through. Only add ¼ cup of nut milk.

2. While the coffee is heating up on the stove, microwave the remaining nut milk for 1 – 3 minutes until hot. Whisk until foamy.

3. Pour coffee into mug and top with whipped nut milk.

Mocha

A creamy coffee topped with a light sprinkle of cocoa powder.

Serves: 2

Prep: 3 minutes

Ingredients:

- 2 cups of brewed coffee, warm
- 1 cup of chocolate almond milk, warm
- Sugar to taste

Ingredients:

1. Combine ingredients in a cup and stir.

Espresso Shot

Perfect for when you need a quick caffeine boost – and tasty too!

Serves: 1

Prep Time: 5 minutes

Ingredients:

- 1 – 3 teaspoons of instant coffee (depending on how strong you like it)
- ½ cup of milk
- ½ cup of water
- 1 ½ teaspoons of sugar (adjust to taste)
- 1/8 teaspoon of cinnamon (optional)
- ¼ teaspoon of cocoa powder (optional)

Ingredients:

1. Combine coffee powder, sugar, cocoa powder and cinnamon in a mug.

2. Add a couple drops of water to turn the mixture into a paste.

3. Combine milk and remaining water in a small saucepan and heat over medium high heat until heated through. Whisk until lightly frothy.

4. Pour into coffee mug.

Iced Vanilla Latte

This iced vanilla latte is sweet and perfectly refreshing. Great for a hot day and to get your daily dose of delicious caffeine.

Serves: 1

Prep Time: 3 minutes

Ingredients:

- ¼ cup brewed coffee
- ½ cup of milk
- ¼ cup vanilla syrup (adjust to taste)
- Ice

Ingredients:

1. Stir all of the ingredients together over ice.

Cold Nutella Coffee

A cold coffee drink with the delicious taste of Nutella and vanilla, I don't think you could ask for much more. Top with whipped cream and melted chocolate to make it even more decadent.

Serves: 2

Prep Time: 4 minutes

Ingredients:

- 2 cups of milk, chilled
- 4 tablespoons of Nutella
- 2 teaspoons of instant coffee
- 2 teaspoons of sugar (adjust to taste)
- 1 teaspoon of vanilla extract

Ingredients:

1. Blend ingredients together in a blender until frothy.

Cinnamon Coconut Latte

This is one of my favourite morning coffees and it may become one of yours too. All the flavours melt together so effortlessly and it's amazing.

Serves: 2

Prep Time: 5 minutes

Ingredients:

- 2 cups of brewed coffee, sweetened with coconut sugar
- ½ cup of coconut milk
- ½ teaspoon of cinnamon
- ¼ teaspoon of vanilla extract
- 1 tablespoon of cocoa powder
- 3 tablespoons of coconut oil

Ingredients:

1. Melt coconut oil in a saucepan over medium-low heat.

2. Stir in cinnamon, vanilla, cocoa powder and milk.

3. Add coffee and allow to rest for 1 minute.

Cinnamon Mocha

This cup of coffee tastes very similar to a cinnamon roll drizzled with chocolate. It's safe to say that this is perfection.

Serves: 2

Prep: 3 minutes

Ingredients:

- 1 cup of brewed coffee, sweetened with 2 tablespoons of maple syrup
- ½ cup of vanilla almond milk
- ½ teaspoon of cinnamon
- ¼ teaspoon of vanilla extract
- 2 tablespoons of chocolate chips
- 2 tablespoons of cocoa powder
- Whipped cream, topping

Ingredients:

1. Melt chocolate chips in a saucepan over medium-low heat.

2. Stir in cinnamon, vanilla, cocoa powder and milk.

3. Add coffee and allow to rest for 1 minute.

Basic Iced Coffee

Recreate that delicious coffee shop iced coffee recipe right in your kitchen.

Serves: 2

Prep Time: 2 minutes

Ingredients:

- 2 teaspoons of instant coffee
- 1 ½ cups of cold water
- 5 tablespoons of half and half cream
- Sugar to taste
- Whipped Cream, topping
- Ice

Ingredients:

1. Dissolve coffee and sugar into water.

2. Fill glass with ice. Add cream to glass and pour coffee on top.

3. Top with whipped cream.

Hot Cocoa Coffee

Nothing is better than combining tasty hot cocoa with coffee, this will certainly hit the spot on a cold day. Top with marshmallows and/or whipped cream.

Serves: 2

Prep Time: 3 minutes

Ingredients:

- 2 cups of milk or water
- 4 tablespoons of cocoa mix
- 2 teaspoons of instant coffee
- 1 teaspoon of cinnamon

Ingredients:

1. Place milk or water in a small saucepan on medium-low heat. Allow to simmer.

2. Add cocoa mix, cinnamon and coffee to mug.

3. Stir in warm liquid.

Coconut Caramel Latte

This drink is like if the tropics melted perfectly with your favourite morning coffee.

Serves: 2

Prep Time: 5 minutes

Ingredients:

- 1 ½ cups of brewed coffee
- ½ cup of coconut milk
- 4 tablespoons of caramel syrup
- 1 teaspoon of sweetened coconut flakes, topping
- Ice

Ingredients:

1. Combine milk, 3 tablespoons of caramel syrup and brewed coffee.

2. Add ice to glass and drizzle in remaining caramel.

3. Top with coconut flakes.

Iced Mocha

An amazing chocolate flavoured coffee brew that you can enjoy on a warm day. Top with whipped cream to make it even better.

Serves: 2

Prep Time: 3 minutes

Ingredients:

- 2 teaspoons of instant coffee
- 2 cups of cold water
- 5 tablespoons of half and half cream
- 4 tablespoons of chocolate syrup
- Sugar to taste
- Whipped Cream, topping (optional)
- Ice

Ingredients:

1. Dissolve coffee and sugar into water. Mix in chocolate syrup.

2. Fill glass with ice. Add cream to glass and pour coffee on top. Mix.

3. Top with whipped cream.

Blended Frozen Mocha

Enjoy a delicious chocolate flavoured coffee in all it's cold, smooth, creamy blended goodness. Top with mini chocolate chips and nuts for even more fun.

Serves: 2

Prep Time: 10 minutes

Ingredients:

- ½ cup of milk
- 1 tablespoon of instant coffee mix
- 2 tablespoons of instant cocoa
- 1 tablespoon of honey or maple syrup
- ½ teaspoon vanilla
- 12 – 16 ice cubes

Ingredients:

1. Combine all ingredients in a blender and blend until smooth.

2. Pour into a chilled glass and drink immediately.

Iced Caramel Latte

Take your instant coffee game up a level with gooey delicious caramel.

Serves: 2

Prep Time: 2 minutes

Ingredients:

- 1 ½ cups of brewed coffee
- ¼ - ½ cup of milk
- 4 tablespoons of caramel syrup
- Whipped cream, topping (optional)
- Ice

Ingredients:

1. Combine milk, 3 tablespoons of caramel syrup and brewed coffee.

2. Add ice to glass, top with whipped cream and drizzle in remaining caramel.

Vanilla Mocha Latte

The place where the delightful flavour of vanilla combines with the smooth, delicious taste of chocolate. Try swapping the milk in this recipe for coconut milk and you'll never turn back.

Serves: 1

Prep Time: 3 minutes

Ingredients:

- 1 cup of brewed coffee
- ¾ cup of milk
- 2 ½ tablespoons of sugar
- ½ tablespoon of vanilla extract
- ½ tablespoon of chocolate syrup
- ½ teaspoon of cinnamon

Ingredients:

1. Combine ingredients in a small saucepan over medium-low heat until mixture is heated through.

2. Top with whipped cream and sprinkle with cinnamon.

Holiday Spice Latte

A delicious warm coffee drink, perfect for the cold holiday season filled with your favourite holiday spices. Topped with whipped cream to make it even better.

Serves: 2

Prep Time: 3 minutes

Ingredients:

- 1 cup of milk
- 1 – 2 tablespoons of sugar
- ¼ teaspoon of ground cloves
- 1 ½ cups of brewed espresso
- ¼ teaspoon of nutmeg
- ¼ teaspoon of ground ginger
- 1/8 teaspoon of orange zest
- ¼ teaspoon cinnamon
- 1/8 teaspoon of lemon zest

Ingredients:

1. Combine ingredients in a small saucepan. Simmer for 1 minute.

2. Allow to slightly cool.

3. Top with whipped cream.

Nutmeg Holiday Coffee

If you've been looking for a drink to start off your holiday mornings, then here's your choice. This drink combines all the memorable flavours of the holiday and the distinct morning coffee taste.

Serves: 2

Prep Time: 10 minutes

Ingredients:

- 2 tablespoons of instant coffee
- 2 cups of water
- ½ of a cinnamon stick
- 1 tablespoon of sugar, adjust to desired sweetness
- ¼ teaspoon of nutmeg
- 1 clove
- 1 teaspoon of orange zest

Ingredients:

1. Add ingredients to a small saucepan and simmer over low-medium heat for 2 minutes. Stir continuously.

2. Turn heat off and steep for 4 minutes.

3. Strain before serving.

Chocolate Coffee Smoothie

Adding coffee to your morning smoothie can help get you going and help you eat (well drink) healthier. This smoothie even serves as a delicious snack when you're feeling a little hungry.

Serves: 2

Prep Time: 5 minutes

Ingredients:

- 3 frozen bananas, cut into chunks
- 2 scoops of chocolate protein powder
- 2 cups of brewed coffee
- 1 cup of vanilla yogurt
- 1 teaspoon vanilla extract
- ½ teaspoon of cinnamon (optional)

Ingredients:

1. Combine ingredients in a blender. Blend until smooth.

Espresso Martini

Coffee plus a cocktail! Delicious espresso and a little chocolate liqueur make quite the pairing.

Serves: 4

Prep Time: 3 minutes

Ingredients:

- ¼ cup of vodka
- 5 tablespoons of espresso coffee - see 'Espresso Shot' recipe.
- 5 tablespoons of coffee liqueur
- Handful of ice

Ingredients:

1. Add ingredients to a cocktail shaker and shake until combined.

2. Strain into chilled cocktail glasses.

Classic Coffee Cake

A delicious moist coffee cake with incredible melted chocolate. Sprinkle with nuts and sweetened coconut flakes and this is a sure pleaser.

Serves: 4

Prep Time: 30 minutes

Ingredients:

- ¼ cup of sugar
- ¼ cup of margarine and 1 tablespoon to grease baking tin
- 1 large egg
- 1 cup self-rising flour
- 1 teaspoon of baking powder
- 1 tablespoon of instant coffee mixed in 1 tablespoon of hot water
- ¼ cup of melted chocolate

Ingredients:

1. Preheat oven to 350 degrees-F. Grease 9-inch cake tin.

2. Whisk together sugar and butter until fluffy.

3. Whisk in egg, and gradually fold in flour and baking powder.

4. Mix in coffee paste until well combined.

5. Bake for 20 – 30 minutes, until done. Allow to cool.

6. Once cool, drizzle with melted chocolate.

Peanut Butter Coffee Mug Cake

The perfect treat when you need something quick and delicious. Peanut butter, coffee and chocolate... there's really no better combo.

Serves: 1

Prep Time: 1 minute

Ingredients:

- 3 tablespoons of flour
- ½ tablespoon of peanut butter
- 1 teaspoon of brewed coffee, or more if you like it strong
- ¼ teaspoon of baking powder
- 1 ½ tablespoon of sugar
- 3 – 5 teaspoons of water
- 1 teaspoon oil
- A pinch of salt

Ingredients:

1. Add oil to mug and coat all sides.

2. Combine ingredients well in a bowl and pour into mug. Microwave for 30 seconds to 1 minute, until done.

3. Top with nuts.

Chocolate Coffee Mug Cake

This mug cake is delectable. Filled with peanuts it has a great crunch and it is very moist because of the condensed milk. You're guaranteed to finish it just as quickly as you made it.

Serves: 1

Prep Time: 1 minute

Ingredients:

- 3 tablespoons of flour
- 2 teaspoons of cocoa powder
- 1 teaspoon of brewed coffee, or more if you like it strong
- 1 teaspoon of condensed milk
- 1 tablespoon of chopped peanuts
- ¼ teaspoon of baking powder
- 1 tablespoon of sugar
- 3 – 5 teaspoons of water
- 1 teaspoon oil
- A pinch of salt

Ingredients:

1. Add oil to mug and coat all sides.

2. Combine ingredients well in a bowl and pour into mug. Microwave for 30 seconds to 1 minute, until done.

Coffee Frosting

This frosting can be had on its own as mousse or serve as a great coffee flavoured whipped cream topping or icing for a cake or muffin.

Yields: 3 cups

Prep Time: 5 minutes

Ingredients:

- 4 cans of coconut milk, full fat
- 3 teaspoons of instant coffee
- 8 tablespoons of powdered sugar
- A pinch of salt

Ingredients:

1. Mix ingredients together using a hand beater or stand mixer until mixture is thick and forms peaks.

2. Use immediately or refrigerate.

Coffee Strawberry Muffins

These muffins are perfect for breakfast. Make a hug batch, freeze them and pop them in the microwave when you're ready.

Yield: 14 muffins

Prep Time: 20 minutes

Ingredients:

- 1 cup of milk
- 2 cups of flour
- 4 teaspoons of baking powder
- ½ cup of sugar
- ¼ teaspoon of salt
- 2 teaspoons of vanilla extract
- 3 tablespoons of oil
- 1 cup of strawberries, diced
- 2 tablespoons of strawberry jam

Ingredients:

1. Preheat oven to 350 degrees-F. Line muffin tin with 14 liners.

2. Whisk together milk, vanilla and oil. Mix in dry ingredients until well combined.

3. Fold in strawberries and swirl in strawberry jam.

4. Spoon batter into muffin liners, filling them half way.

5. Bake for 20 minutes, until they have risen and are baked through.

6. Allow to cook for 10 minutes before removing from tin.

Microwave Coffee and Walnut Cake

You can make a moist, delicious full cake right in your microwave in no time. This cake serves 4 people and is a great treat during breakfast, or lunch... or whatever time of day you prefer really.

Serves: 4

Prep Time: 10 minutes

Ingredients:

- ¼ cup soft butter, room temperature
- ¼ cup of sugar
- 2 eggs
- ¼ cup of self-rising flour
- 2 teaspoons of instant coffee powder
- 1 teaspoon of nutmeg
- ½ teaspoon of cinnamon
- 1 cup of walnuts, chopped
- ¼ teaspoon of salt
- Buttercream
- 1 teaspoon of instant coffee powder
- 1 teaspoon of milk
- 2 tablespoons of room temperature butter
- ½ cup of icing sugar
- ½ teaspoon of vanilla

Ingredients:

1. Beat butter and sugar together into a bowl. Once fluffy, add eggs and beat until smooth.

2. Mix in flour, cinnamon, nutmeg, coffee, salt and walnuts until well combined.

3. Transfer to a microwave proof baking dish and microwave for 3 – 5 minutes until done.

4. For icing, whisk together ingredients until smooth and fluffy.

5. Allow cake to cook and top with icing.

Coffee Ice Cream

Smooth, creamy coffee ice cream that is simply amazing on a hot day. No ice cream machine needed!

Serving size: 2 pints

Prep Time: 10 minutes

Ingredients:

- 4 cups of heavy whipping cream, cold
- 4 cups of sweetened condensed milk, cold
- 4 teaspoons of vanilla extract
- ¼ cup of brewed coffee

Method:

1. Whip the cold heavy whipping cream in a stand mixer or with a hand beater until soft peaks are formed.

2. Add the condensed milk to the cream and continue whipping until stiff peaks are formed. Fold in vanilla extract and brewed coffee.

3. Scoop mixture into an air-tight container. Freeze for at least 6 hours.

Chocolate Coffee Ice Cream

Crunchy, cold amazing no churn ice cream. Super easy to make and oh so tasty. Filled with nuts and chocolate chips, this is one of my all-time favourites.

Serving size: 2 pints

Prep Time: 10 minutes

Ingredients:

- 4 cups of heavy whipping cream, cold
- 4 cups of sweetened condensed milk, cold
- 4 teaspoons of vanilla extract
- ¼ cup of brewed coffee
- ¼ cup of peanuts, chopped
- 1 teaspoon of cocoa powder
- ¼ cup of mini chocolate chips

Method:

1. Whip the cold heavy whipping cream in a stand mixer or with a hand beater until soft peaks are formed.

2. Add the condensed milk and cocoa powder to the cream and continue whipping until stiff peaks are formed. Fold in vanilla extract, peanuts, chocolate chips and brewed coffee.

3. Scoop mixture into an air-tight container. Freeze for at least 6 hours.

Coffee Caramel Fudge

This is a tasty treat that only needs a few ingredients. It melts right in your mouth and can be customized with so many things; peanut butter and sweetened coconut flakes are my personal favourites.

Serving size: 10

Cooking time: 5 minutes

Ingredients:

- 4 cups of chocolate chips, melted
- 4 cups of condensed milk, cold
- 2 teaspoons of vanilla extract
- 2 cups of caramel sauce

Method:

1. Combine melted chocolate chips and condensed milk in a microwave safe bowl. Microwave for 30 seconds and stir until well combined.

2. Mix in caramel sauce and fold in vanilla.

3. Grease a baking pan with butter or cooking spray and pour mixture into baking pan.

4. Refrigerate for at least an hour and cut into small squares.

Coffee Cocktail

A mysterious looking drink that's got a nice kick to it and a crisp burn from the espresso and ginger beer.

Serves: 2

Prep Time: 5 minutes

Ingredients:

- 4 tablespoons of brewed espresso
- 2 cups of ginger beer
- 3 tablespoons of dark rum
- 3 tablespoons of tequila
- Ice

Ingredients:

1. Fill glasses with ice and pour in the rum, tequila and ginger beer. Stir.

2. Slowly pour in espresso.

Mocha Milkshake

A delicious creamy, chocolate-y milkshake with just a hint of coffee flavour. You can try topping these with cherries, chocolate syrup and chocolate sprinkles!

Serves: 2

Prep Time: 5 minutes

Ingredients:

- 1 cup of milk chocolate chips
- 2 teaspoons of instant coffee
- 1 ½ cups of milk
- 2 scoops of vanilla ice cream
- ¼ teaspoon of vanilla extract

Ingredients:

1. Combine all of the ingredients in a blender.

2. Blend until smooth. Not too long or it will get warm.

Conclusion

There you have it! Now it's time for you to change your mornings forever with delicious, coffee shop quality (and better) mixes made right in your kitchen.

I hope these recipes will help you to discover how amazing coffee can be and how creative you can be in the kitchen. You can begin mixing up coffee concoctions on your own in no time!

Dear Reader,

Thank you very much for choosing my book. I hope you really enjoy it. If don't mind I would like to ask you to leave a review after reading.

Thanks.

Sincerely yours,

Stephanie Sharp

For announcements about new releases,

please follow my author page on

Amazon.com! (Look for the Follow Bottom

under the photo) You can find that at

https://www.amazon.com/author/stephanie-sharp

or Scan QR-code below.